Lectora® 11 Upgrade Guide

This book is a guide solely for Lectora 8, 9, and X users. It gives a quick overview of Lectora 11 along with:

- Where they moved stuff from X to 11
- What's new and what has changed
- What they took away and what doesn't work quite like you would expect

About the Author

Ben Pitman has been developing courses in Lectora for over 8 years. He has helped thousands of people with Lectora problems on the community forum and is known there as "Dr. Lectora." He has written many books on Lectora and has developed many "add-ons".

Other Books by Benjamin Pitman
Paperback on Amazon
    Designing Effective eLearning: A Step-by-Step Guide Ed. 1.3 (2013)
    Lectora 201: What They Don't Tell You in Class (due late 2013)
    Lectora 301: Techniques for Professionals (due mid 2013)
    Business Process Reengineering: Plain and Simple (1990)

To my sister Bonnie,

Who is always "upgrading" her life
despite world-class challenges.

As always, thanks to the Trivantis staff
without whom this book would not have
been possible.

Lectora 11 Upgrade Guide

Edition 1.2

May 2013

Benjamin Pitman, Ph.D.
a.k.a. Dr. Lectora

© Copyright 2013 by Benjamin Pitman. All rights reserved.

eProficiency, Inc.
1810 Chattahoochee Run Drive
Suwanee, GA 30024
678-571-4179
www.eProficiency.com

No part of this publication may be reproduced, stored in a retrieval system, or transmitted in any form or by any means, electronic, mechanical, photocopying, recording, scanning, or otherwise, except as permitted under Section 107 or 108 of the 1976 United States Copyright Act, without the prior written permission of the Author. Requests to the Author for permission should be addressed to the Permissions Department, eProficiency, Inc. 1810 Chattahoochee Run Dr., Suwanee, GA 30024, 678-571-4179, email: support@eproficiency.com.

Limit of Liability/Disclaimer of Warranty: While the publisher and the author have used their best efforts in preparing this document, they make no representations or warranties with respect to accuracy or completeness of the contents of this document and specifically disclaim any implied warranties of merchantability or fitness for a particular purpose. The advice and strategies contained herein may not be suitable to your situation. You should consult with a professional where appropriate. Neither the publisher nor the author shall be liable for any loss of profit or any other commercial damages, including but not limited to special, incidental, consequential, or other damages.

For general information on other products and services including training and coaching, or technical support, please visit www.eProficiency.com or contact Ben Pitman at 678-571-4179, support@eProficiency.com.

Trademarks: Lectora is a registered trademark of Trivantis Corporation. Windows®, Microsoft®, Microsoft® Word®, and PowerPoint® are registered trademarks of Microsoft® Corporation. Flash® is a registered trademark of Adobe Systems Inc. Other product and company names mentioned herein may be the trademarks of their respective owners. Use of trademarks or product names is not intended to convey endorsement or affiliation with this book.

Library of Congress Cataloging-in-Publication Data

Pitman, Benjamin.

Lectora 11 Upgrade Guide

Includes index.

ISBN-13: 978-1484980835

ISBN-10: 1484980832

1. Lectora. 2. Computer-based training development. 3. Authoring tools. 4. Authoring Applications. 5. Web-based training development.

Contents

1. Introduction—1
    Goal of This Book—1
    What This Book Does *Not* Cover—1
    Prerequisites—1

  Organization of This Book—2

  The Lectora File Structure—2

  Other Resources—2
    Learn More about *Development* in Lectora:—2
    Learn More about *Designing* E-Learning—3
    Get Help Designing and Developing Courses—3

2. Where's My Stuff?—5
  What's on the Screen—5
    Menus—7
    Toolbars to Ribbons—8
    Properties Tabs—8
    Getting Help—9

3. What's New or Changed?—11
  General Change—11

  Customizing Your Lectora Interface—11
    Adding Items to the Quick Access Toolbar—12
    Creating Shortcut Keys—12
    Setting Your Save Options—13

  Action Ribbon—13
    Description Field—13
    Action Pane—14
    New Triggers—14
    New or Changed Actions—15

  File Tab—16

  Design Ribbon—16

  Home Ribbon—16
    Setting Color—17

- Insert Ribbon—17
    - Smart Text—18
    - Tables—18
    - Characters—20
    - Shapes/Lines—21
    - Audio and Video—22
    - Flash Animations (SWFs)—26
    - YouTube—27
    - Buttons—27
    - Table of Contents—28
    - Menus—29
    - Progress Bar—30
    - Timer—30
    - Web Window—31
    - Social Media—31
    - HTML Extension—31
    - QR Code—32
- Lectora Library—32
- Position & Size Ribbon—33
- Properties—33
- Test & Survey Ribbon—33
    - Choice Properties Common to Most Questions—34
    - Drag and Drop Questions—34
    - Hot Spot Questions—35
    - Fill in the Blank Questions—35
    - Matching Questions—36
    - Multiple Choice Questions—37
    - Multiple Response Questions—38
    - Number Entry Questions—38
    - Rank/Sequence Questions—39
    - Question Feedback—39
    - Restricting the Number of Attempts—40
- Test Properties Ribbon—41
- Test Behavior Ribbon—41
- Test Results Ribbon—42
- Tools Ribbon—43
    - Recording Audio—43
    - Recording Video—43
- View Ribbon—44
    - Modes—44
    - Grids and Guides—44

Refresh the Page—45
Moveable and Dockable Panes—45

4. What Is the Downside?—47
What Did They Take Away?—47
What Doesn't Work As Expected or Needed—48

Index—51

1. Introduction

Here's how this book came about. I got Lectora 11 and realized I had to completely rewrite my old version of Lectora 101. In doing so, I had to figure out most of the new features. So, I thought that putting this all together for experienced people so they could make the transition easier might be of use to some Lectora users. Hope it is for you.

Goal of This Book

The goal of this book is simple – to help you get a jump start using the new version of Lectora. It has a lot of new features and some definite improvements.

What This Book Does *Not* Cover

- Details of any specific technique
- How to use Lectora in detail

Prerequisites

This book is about Lectora 11 and the changes from Lectora X and previous versions.

- You should be familiar Lectora X.
- If you still are working on 8 or 9, you will likely find some new things as you use Lectora 11. I did not try to cover all the improvements from 8 to 9 or 9 to X.6.

Organization of This Book

Just three chapters covering what most people want to know.

Where's My Stuff?	The first thing most of us want to know when we open an upgrade is "Where is …?" They always move stuff around and it takes a while to find it. So this first chapter is devoted to helping you find your stuff. Some things have changed the way they work and many have improvements. The next chapter covers these.
What's New?	Next thing we want to know of course is "What's new?" This chapter covers what has changed or improved and what is brand new.
What's the Downside?	Okay, "there ain't no free lunch." A couple of things have gone by the way side or no longer work as they used to. And you may find some things that are not to your liking. I have identified as many as I could find and given workarounds.

The Lectora File Structure

As far as I can tell, there has been no change to the Lectora file structure and what files and folders are created.

Other Resources

This book covers the fundamentals of creating an e-learning course using Lectora. There are other books and online resources that you can use.

Learn More about *Development* in Lectora:

• *Lectora 201: What They Don't Teach You in Class* by Ben Pitman • *Lectora 301: Techniques for Professionals* by Ben Pitman • *Lectora 401: Creating Your Own Games* by Ben Pitman • Other Lectora books can be found by searching Amazon.	E-books for Lectora 8, 9, X available at www.eProficiency.com in the Knowhow Store Lectora 11 versions in paperback due out on Amazon in 2013

• Free tutorials, tips, toolkit, and other free things to read and expand Lectora	www.eProficiency.com/webStore/ www.quizzicle.com www.artisanelearning.com
• Add-ons and techniques for some price	www.eProficiency.com/webStore/ www.quizzicle.com
• Free webinars, demos, tutorials, how-to courses, sample courses, and white papers	www.Lectora.com > LectoraU
• Training and product user guides	www.Lectora.com > Support

Learn More about *Designing* E-Learning

• *Designing Effective e-Learning: A Step-by-Step Guide*	Amazon.com
• *Designing Scenario Based Courses* (for any tool)	E-book available at www.eProficiency.com in the Know-how Store Paper back due out on Amazon in 2014
• Recommended books	www.eProficiency.com > Recommended Books
• Free tutorials	www.eProficiency.com/webStore/ and click on Instr. Design category

Get Help Designing and Developing Courses

These developers all have a solid knowledge of designing courses for e-learning and development in Lectora:

- Ben Pitman (Dr. Lectora) for free advice as well as paid services at www.eProficiency.com
- Jay Lambert at www.integratedlearnings.com
- Diane Elkins at www.artisanelearning.com
- Peter Sorenson at www.quizzicle.com
- Ron Wincek at www.interactiveadvantage.com

2. Where's My Stuff?

The big challenge when you first start using Lectora 11 is to figure out where all the tools you used before are now. This section shows you where most of your tools have moved to in Lectora 11.

What's on the Screen

On the below is the basic Lectora screen. If you are using Microsoft® Office 2007 or 2010, some of this should already look familiar.

- Across the top you will see the **Quick Access Toolbar**. It is customizable just like the ones in MS Office. You can add icons (buttons) for things you do frequently.
- Below that are the tabs that get you to the various ribbons. These are similar to those in MS Office applications. Each ribbon is composed of groups of icons (buttons) that perform various functions. These replace the menus in previous versions of Lectora.

You can press **Ctrl+F1** to collapse the ribbon if you need the space. You can press **Ctrl+F1** again to expand it.

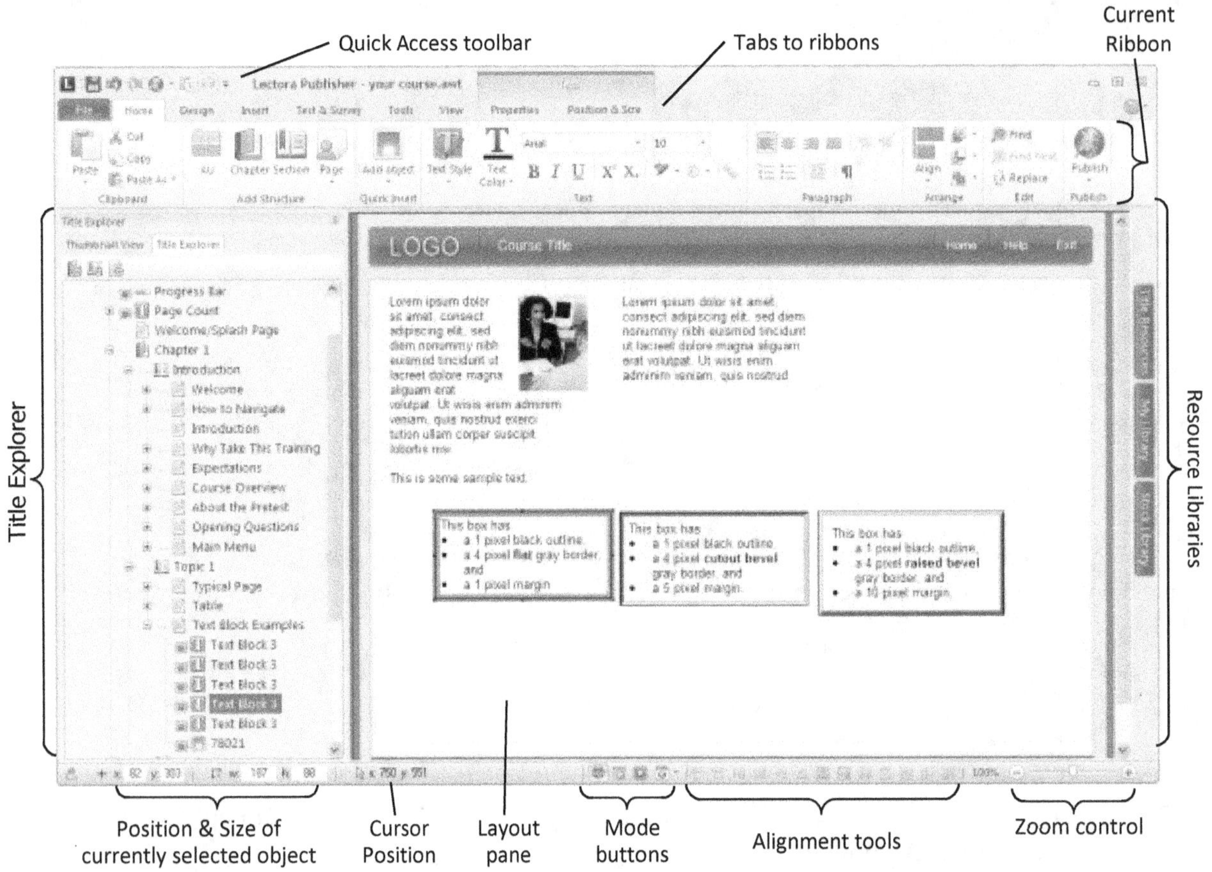

2. Where's My Stuff?

[Screenshot of Lectora Publisher interface with labeled callouts: Quick Access toolbar, Tabs to ribbons, Current Ribbon, Title Explorer, Resource Libraries, Position & Size of currently selected object, Cursor Position, Layout pane, Mode buttons, Alignment tools, Zoom control]

You can get to your resources including the Lectora Library using the tabs on the right.

Some of the items in the status bar have moved and you now have Mode buttons and Alignment tools here. The RGB color at the curser seems to be gone.

 **Warning 1:** If your Lectora window is not wide enough, many of the ribbons will *not* look like what you see in this book. Different ribbons need different amounts of space. You should expand the window as wide as it will go and then close it back up until just before groups start compressing.

The icons in the Title Explorer have changed but they are still easily recognizable.

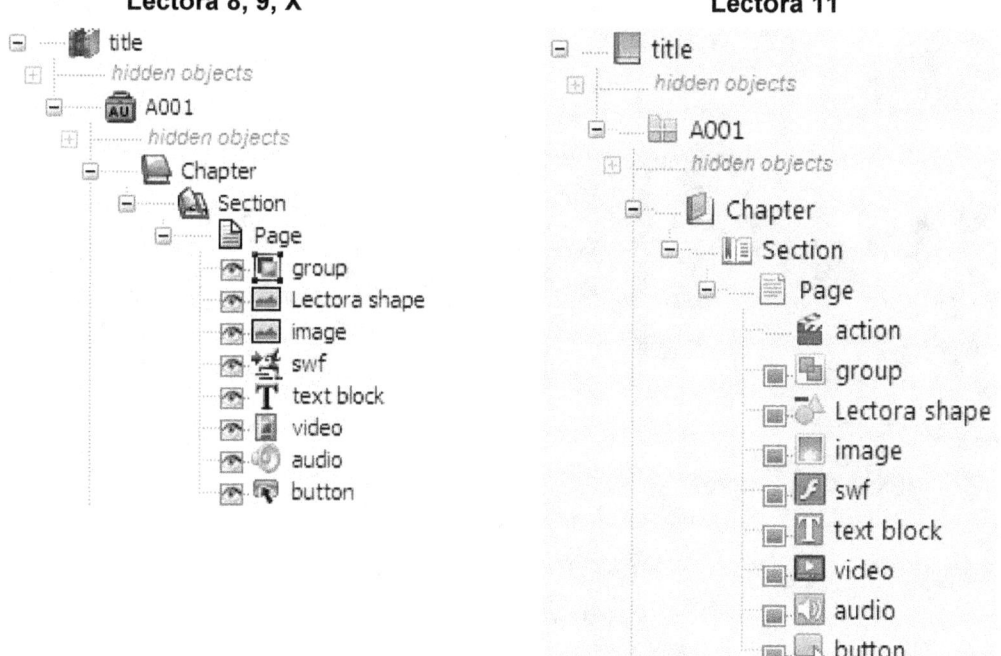

Menus

File menu	→	File ribbon
Edit menu	→	Home ribbon
Add menu	→	Insert ribbon or the Add Object icon on the Home ribbon
Layout menu	→	Home ribbon > Arrange group
Tools menu	→	Tools ribbon
Mode menu	→	View ribbon > Modes group
Publish menu	→	Home ribbon > Publish group or from same icon on Quick Access Toolbar
View menu	→	View ribbon
Preferences Grids & Guides	→	View ribbon
Lectora Library	→	My Library on right side of window

Toolbars to Ribbons

Properties Tabs

Most common properties are now on the Properties ribbon. The Position and Size tab now has its own ribbon. If there was not room on the Properties ribbon for other properties, then additional ribbons are shown when the object is selected.

The HTML name of objects is found by first turning on the preference

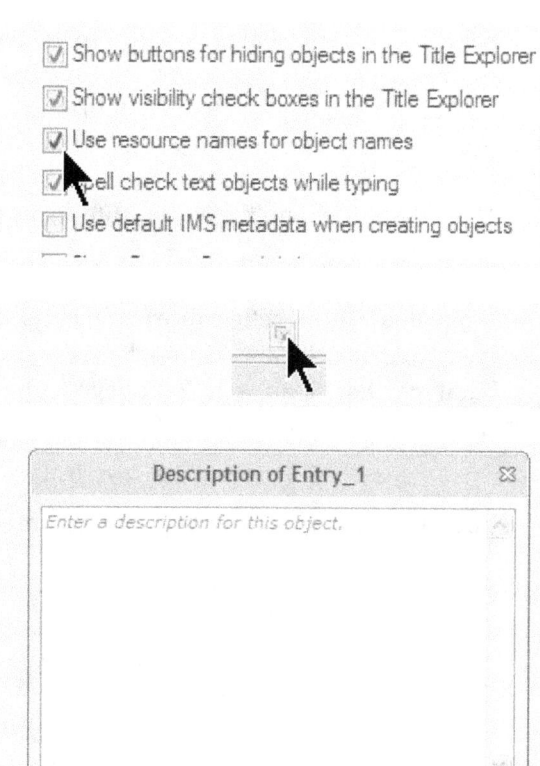

and then going to the object's Properties and clicking on the diagonal arrow in the lower right corner of the first group.

This brings up the Description window and at the bottom you will find the object's HTML name.

Getting Help

The makers of Lectora have provided a wealth of help with this version of Lectora.

You can click on the question mark icon in the upper right corner of the Lectora window.

On many ribbons, you will this icon on the right. Click it for detailed information on the tools on that ribbon.

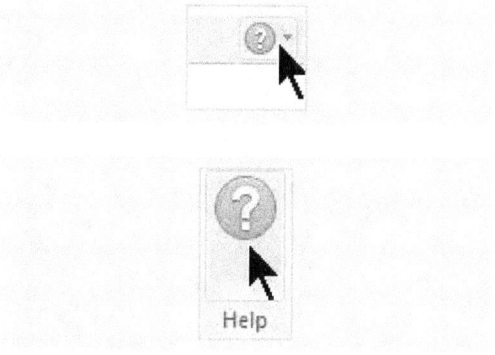

Some tools open a dialog window. In the bottom right of the window you will see a Help button. You can click it to get help on that dialog window.

The video editor and the audio editor have their own Help available when the editors are open.

If you don't see a Help button, just press the F1 key.

While this built-in help is nice and handy, sometimes I have had trouble finding what I want. I have had better luck searching the User Guide PDF. One is installed when you installed Lectora but it may not be current. You can go to the folder where Lectora was installed and create a shortcut to it. For Lectora Professional on Windows® XP, the file is located here.

  "C:\Program Files\Trivantis\Lectora Publisher\Docs\Lectora_User_Guide.pdf"

You can go to www.Lectora.com > Support and find the current PDF.

3. What's New or Changed?

There are many ways to approach this topic. What seemed best is to just tackle the ribbons one at a time and go through them pointing out what has changed significantly in function. We will not cover things that have simply changed in appearance. Again, this book is for experienced Lectora users who are trying to get a jump-start on Lectora 11.

The ribbons are covered in alphabetical order. Anything else got crazy. I did combine a few that seemed to belong together like the Menu and Submenu ribbons. Also, if there was something different about the properties, I covered them at the time I was covering the object so you will find properties scattered throughout.

General Change

In X, some actions and objects had a small window available or maybe you clicked and Edit button to change the text or coordinates you wanted to enter.

In 11, look for an Edit pencil somewhere on the Properties ribbon. Here are a couple of examples.

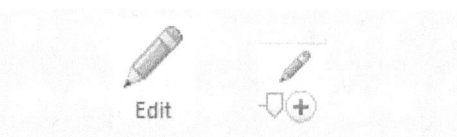

Customizing Your Lectora Interface

The ways to customize your Lectora interface has changed slightly.

Adding Items to the Quick Access Toolbar

You are probably familiar with this as it is very similar to MS Office products. You can put icons you want here that you use frequently.

If you do something a lot, it may be quicker to add it to the Quick Access Toolbar.

Right click on any ribbon and select Customize Quick Access Toolbar...

In the dialog window that appears, use the dropdown lists to select items to add to the Quick Access Toolbar.

Lectora 11 Tip 1: Move the Quick Access Toolbar to below the ribbon to make it closer to your layout area. Do this in all your MS Office apps. It takes a couple of days to get used to this but once you do, the things you use all the time are much closer at hand.

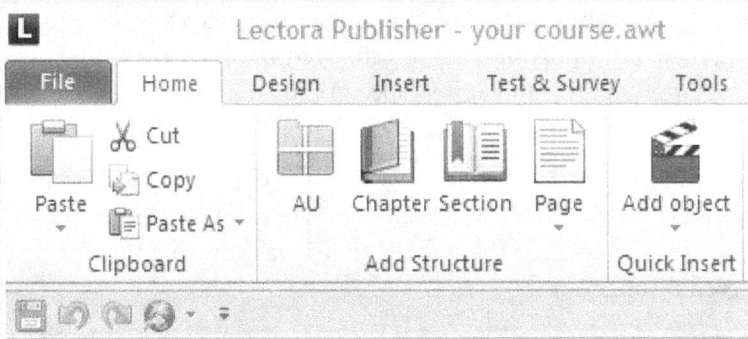

Creating Shortcut Keys

Some people like to set up their own shortcut keys. These are now set as below instead of from Preferences as before.

1. Right click on any ribbon and select Customize Quick Access Toolbar...

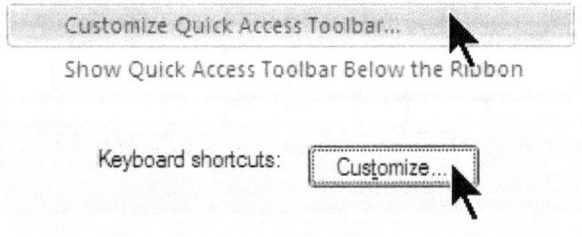

2. Near the bottom of the dialog window you will see Keyboard shortcuts. Click on the Customize... button and create shortcuts.

Setting Your Save Options

This has moved from Preferences to the File tab.

1. On the File tab, click Save Options.

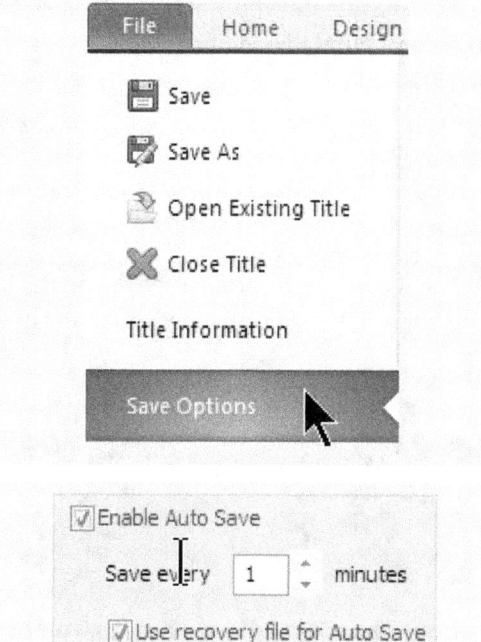

2. At the bottom, check Enable Auto Save and set it to save every 1 minute.

Action Ribbon

The Action ribbon is a replacement for the old action properties. This like many of the other ribbons is dynamic, that is it changes depending on what action the action is.

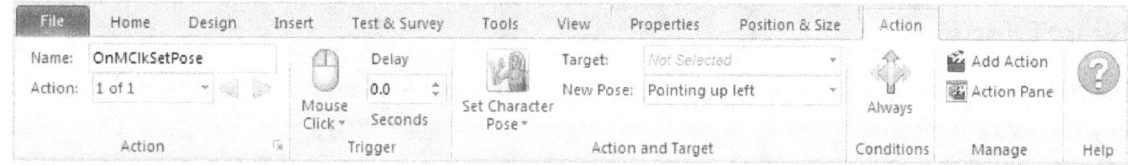

Description Field

In the lower right of the first part of the ribbon is a diagonal arrow.

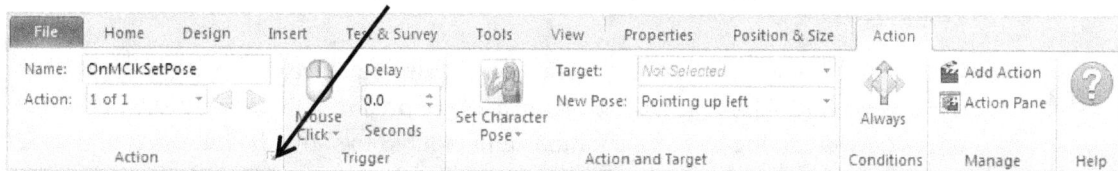

When you click it you can enter a description for the action.

Lectora 11 Tip 2: Use this to document your more complex actions.

Action Pane

You can easily see all the actions attached to an object and what they do by:

- first clicking on one of its actions,
- then clicking on Action Pane on the Action ribbon.

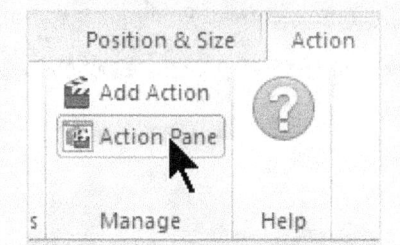

This will display the Action Pane below the layout area. Here you will see the name of the object to which the actions are attached and a list of the actions.

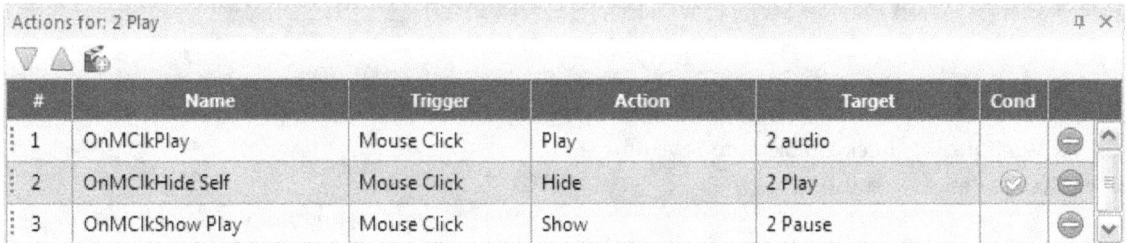

- If you want to add more actions, you can click on the Add Action icon here as well as other places on ribbons.
- You can click on any of them and make changes in the Action ribbon.
- You can change the order in which they run by clicking on one and then click on the green arrows to move them up to run earlier or down to run later.
- You can delete them by clicking the ⊖ on the right.

New Triggers

There is one new trigger, On Page Show. This allows you to put Page level actions attached to an object so they happen sooner.

> **Lectora 11 Tip 3:** Attach actions that change text boxes and graphics when the page shows *directly* to the objects instead of at the page level. It will make your code easier to understand and a lot easier to exclude things like the page count because you only have to exclude the text box. The actions are already attached to it.

 **Warning 2:** If you want actions to run in a certain sequence, it is better to put them all on one object or on the page instead of spreading them around. Suppose you were doing some calculations and wanted to show the intermediate results in one text box and the final results in another. You might be tempted to split them between the two text boxes using On Page Show. The problem is that the results (which depend on the intermediate actions) may run first.

New or Changed Actions

Action	Description of Change
Display Message	Now you have a nice big window to enter your text into.
Display Page in Popup	This is the old Display Message in a Custom Message Window.
Go To Web Address	This is now a standalone action. You have a nice big window to enter your URL in now.
Modify Variable	When you click the diagonal arrow in the Value field, you now have buttons at the bottom that allow you to select variables from the course or specify a random value. **Lectora 11 Tip 4:** You can now easily build strings by simply putting them in all at once. Here is an example of creating the page numbering. In Lectora X it this single action took 4 actions. Value `Page VAR(PageInChapter) of VAR(PagesInChapter)` No, sorry, you can't do math this way.
Open Attachment	Display a document like a PDF in a new window.
Launch a Document	Open a document in its native application like MS Word®. Not sure how this differs from Open Attachment above.
Resize	This is the new name for the old SizeTo action.
Run JavaScript	This is now a much easier way to run JavaScript. Just enter it into the window.
Set Character Pose	This works with the new pose-able characters and allows you to easily change the poses of the predefined characters.
Tin Can Statement	This action lets you do Tin Can stuff but I have not had an opportunity to do any of that so I can't help you much with it.

File Tab

Here are the few things I have found that have changed on the File tab.

The Title Information tab gives the usual information about the file. It also allows you to Enable Author Control and enter a password. Then any object can be protected by clicking the

Author Control 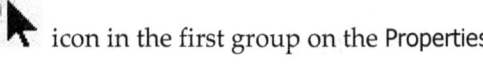 icon in the first group on the Properties ribbon.

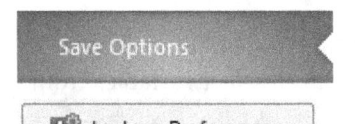

The Save options gives you the usual selections. Save options are here now instead of in Preferences.

Nothing new. A few things have moved to other locations to be more like MS Office.

Author Control is now on the Title Information tab.

Save Options have their own tab.

Keyboard shortcut is now on found at the bottom of the window when you right click on a ribbon and select Customize Quick Access Toolbar.

Design Ribbon

The Design ribbon lets you set the characteristics (properties) of the entire course. This is the old Title properties.

You can now apply themes to your course if you want to use the standard graphics. Nice for creating a prototype but unlikely to be used in a production course because you will likely have your own color scheme and graphics.

Home Ribbon

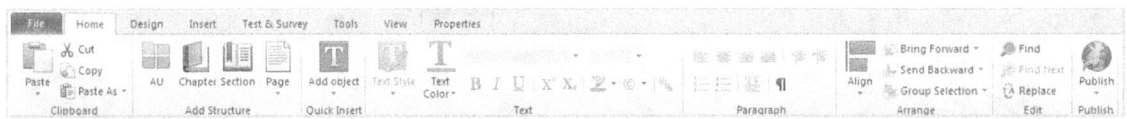

The Home ribbon provides most of the usual functions allowing you to cut, copy, paste, add the more common items like Chapters and Pages, as well as format and layer text.

The **Paste** text icon will remember if you are pasting unformatted.

The **Add Object** icon changes to reflect your most recent object that you added. The new and changed objects are covered when we discuss the Insert ribbon.

Setting Color

You can apply text color using the pallet.

Now it automatically remembers the 16 most recently used colors.

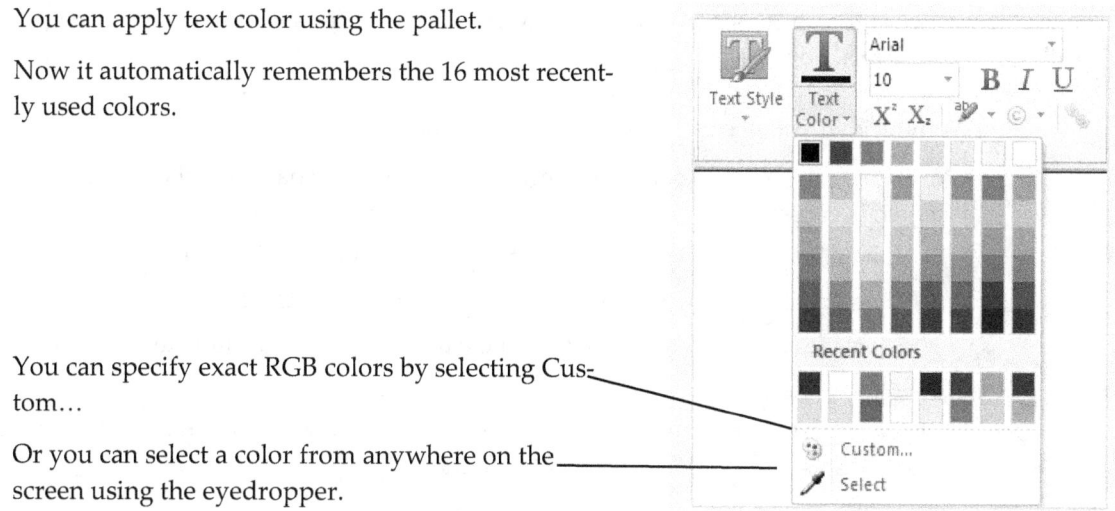

You can specify exact RGB colors by selecting Custom…

Or you can select a color from anywhere on the screen using the eyedropper.

Insert Ribbon

The **Insert** ribbon is a replacement for the old **Add** menu and the old **Insert** toolbar. Let's look and the new and changed objects. These are covered in the order in which they appear on the ribbon rather than in alphabetic order.

Smart Text

Four new additions are known as "smart text". The Page Number replaces the old Page Numbering Tool.

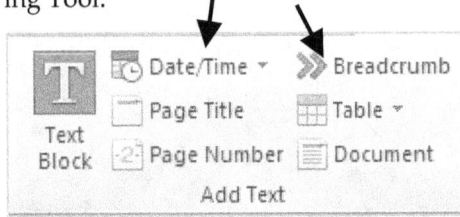

Just click on one, select the options if any, and you are done. A text box is inserted onto the page with all the appropriate actions.

Warning 3: If you use this object, be aware of the following.

- It is generally a good idea to use reasonably short page names in the Title Explorer, because:
  - long names can be difficult to read if you have a table of contents and
  - long names can cause horizontal scrolling in the Title Explorer.

  For these reasons, you may want the page title and the page name to be different.

- If you export the course to MS Word®, the pages are not labeled in the exported text – that is, they will not have a title on them.
- If you print your course to a PDF, the pages will not be labeled.
- And most important, *spell check does not check the names* in the Title Explorer because many people use abbreviations.

Tables

Tables are much easier to create now. Click on the Table icon in either:

- the Add Text group on the Insert ribbon or

- the Add group on the Text Properties ribbon.

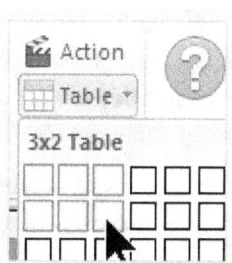

Lectora 11 Tip 5: Unfortunately, right now, the Insert ribbon creates a new text box. If you want a table in an existing text box, click and get your cursor where it should be in the box and then right click and select Table.

Once you click inside the table, a new tab for the Table ribbon will appear.

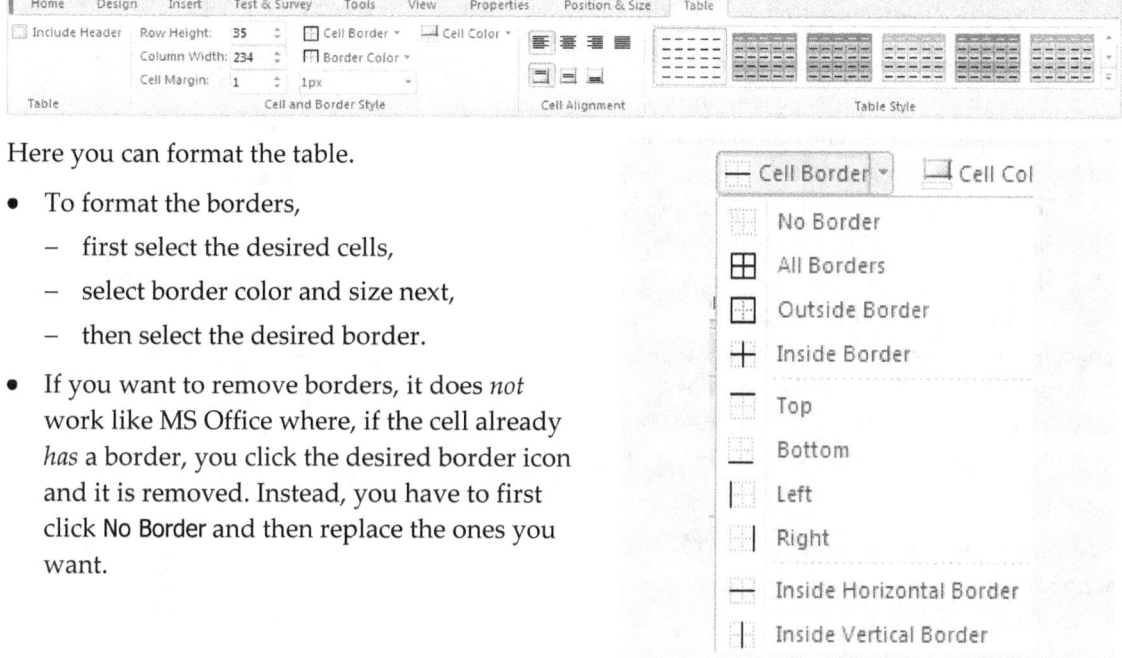

Here you can format the table.

- To format the borders,
    - first select the desired cells,
    - select border color and size next,
    - then select the desired border.
- If you want to remove borders, it does *not* work like MS Office where, if the cell already *has* a border, you click the desired border icon and it is removed. Instead, you have to first click No Border and then replace the ones you want.

The Include Header property is for web-based 508 compliance. See Lectora Help for more details.

On this ribbon, you can set a fixed row height, column width, border size, color, cell fill color, and objects are aligned in the cell. You can select more than one cell at a time and apply these properties. You select one of the preformatted table styles – a nice addition to Lectora 11.

Finally, you can insert rows, columns, merge cells, split cells, and delete cells from the Edit Table dropdown list. They are only available when your cursor is in a table ready to enter text.

These functions are also available by right clicking when in a table and selecting Table.

Characters

Use "pose-able" characters to make your point.

Lectora now provides a whole host of characters with some 15 different poses each. These can be used as simple avatars. They have the following poses:

1. Arms crossed
2. Happy
3. OK Sign
4. Pointing down left
5. Pointing down right
6. Pointing middle left
7. Pointing middle right
8. Pointing up left
9. Pointing up right
10. Sad
11. Thinking
12. Thumbs Down
13. Thumbs Up
14. Waving
15. Writing

You can change the pose using a Set Character Pose action. Like any other special effect, be careful not to over use it.

1. Click on the Character icon on the Insert ribbon.

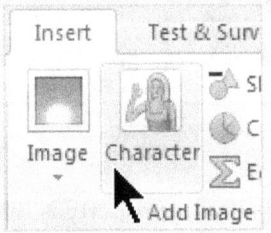

2. This will open the Stock Library. Browse around and find an appropriate character.

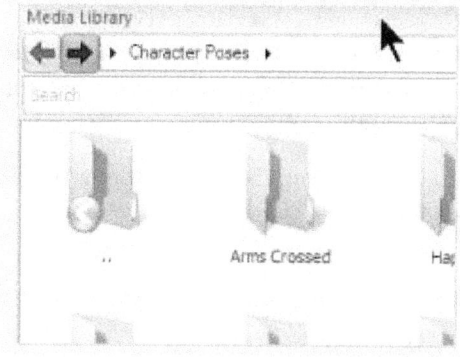

3. Then when you need to change the pose, use a Set Character Pose action.

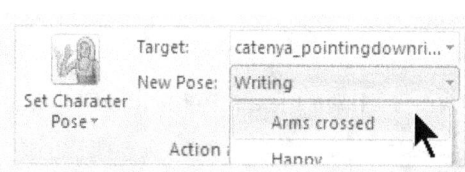

Shapes/Lines

Shapes and lines are found under this tool.

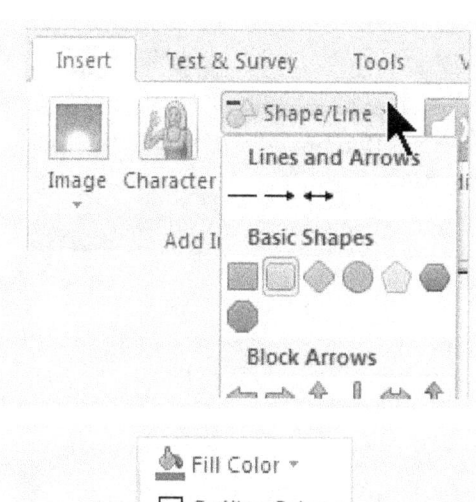

To change the color, or outline properties, click on the shape and then on the Properties ribbon. Change the shape's color and size in the Style group.

One big improvement is that now, if you resize a shape, the outline *stays the same and does not stretch*.

Audio and Video

You can insert streaming media as well as regular media files. When you select the Streaming, you enter the URL of the desired media.

You can still drag the media from a Windows folder onto the page.

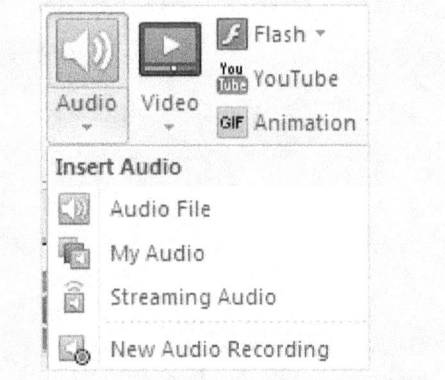

Once you have the audio file inserted and selected, you have access to the audio **Properties**.

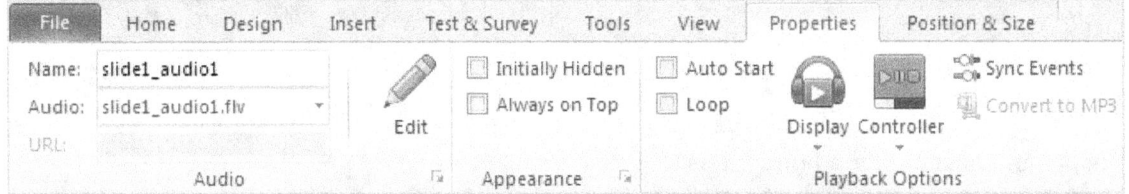

If you want to change the media file used, you can select a different audio file using the Audio or Video dropdown box.

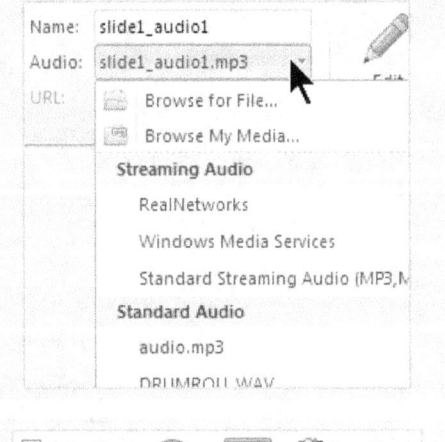

Now, make your selections in the Playback Options group.

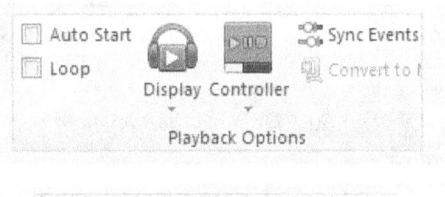

You can convert media files to MP3 or MP4 from the Properties ribbon.

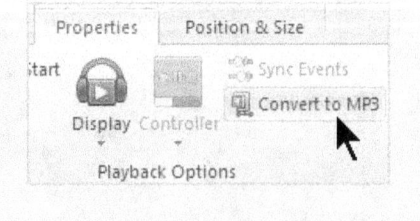

Editing Audio

When you click on the Edit button on its Properties ribbon or right click on the audio object and select Edit, it brings up an audio file editor where you can:

- cut and paste parts of the audio,
- fade parts in or out,
- adjust the volume,
- insert silence, or
- add events.

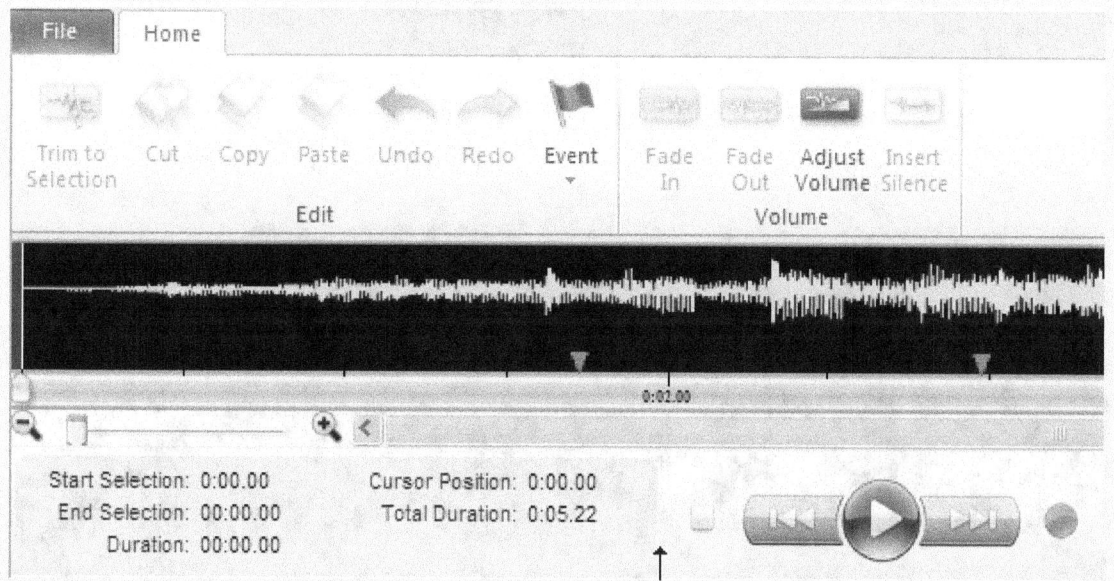

To select a portion of the audio, simply click in the black area and drag your cursor. You can also hold the Shift key down and click. The area selected will be from the current play position to where you clicked.

Once you have a selected area, you can delete everything but the selection using Trim to Selection. You can Cut, Copy, Fade, Adjust Volume, or silence the recording.

The editor is easier to use than previous versions.

Adding Events

1. There are several ways to do this. You can right click on the object and select Edit, click the Edit icon on its Properties ribbon, or probably the easiest is to click on the Sync Events icon in the Playback Options group on its Properties ribbon. This will open the Synchronize Events dialog box.

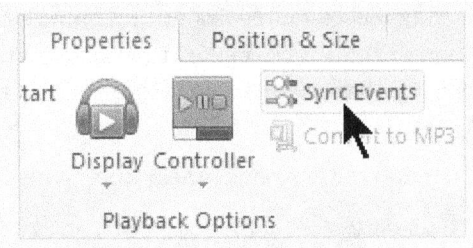

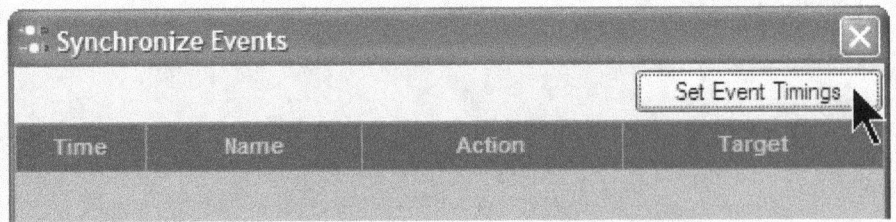

2. Click on the Set Event Timings button to open the media editor.

   When the media editor opens, you will see the media and a timeline.

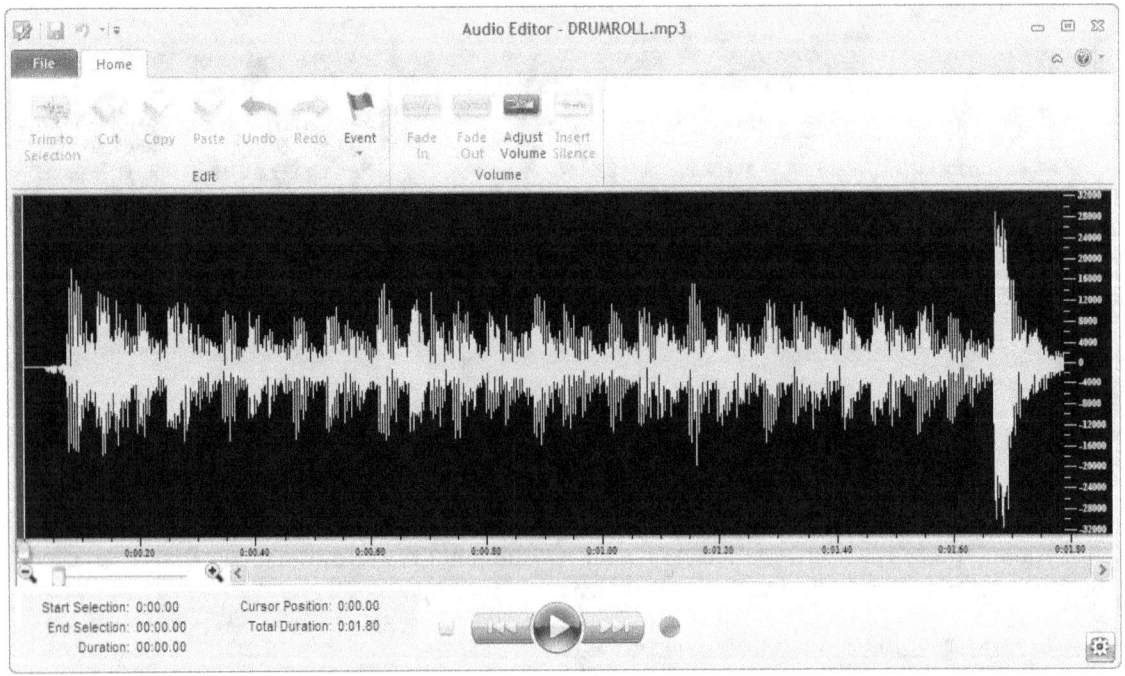

3. Play the media to the point where you want something to happen. Click Pause.

4. Click the Event icon in the media editor's Home ribbon.

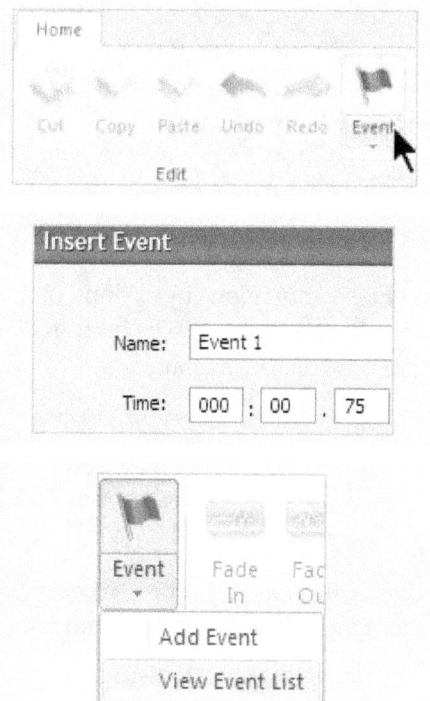

5. The Event dialog window will open to confirm your event. Click OK. A red arrow will appear on the timeline where the event is.

6. If you want to change the time of an event or delete it, click on the Event icon and select Event List from the dropdown list.

    When the Event List opens, you can click on an event and then change the time or name or remove it.

7. Save your changes and close the editor.

Adding Actions to Events

Now the Synchronize Events dialog window should look something like this with the events showing but nothing happening (no actions).

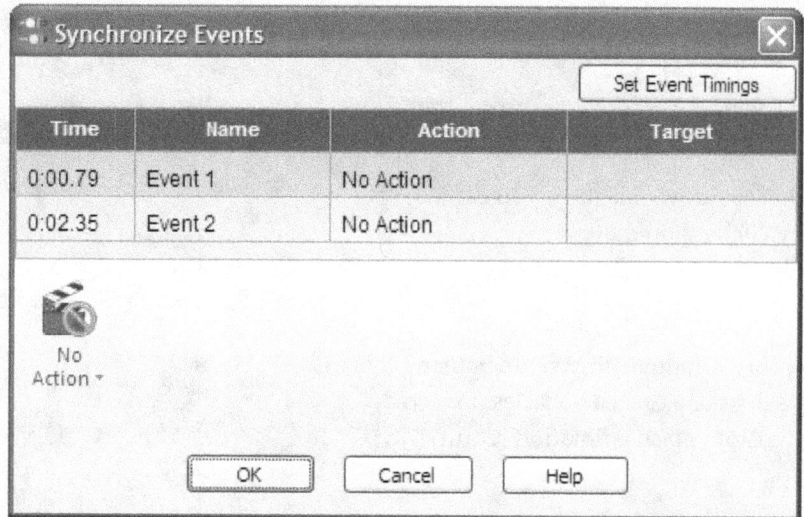

Click on an event to select it and then click the action icon in the lower part of the window. Initially they are all set to No Action. Change the action to do what you want.

Flash Animations (SWFs)

Insert Flash animations by clicking on the Flash icon on the Insert ribbon. The built-in Flash activities are now readily available

1. Check the Transparent property if you have anything you want to show through the Flash object like a start or stop button.

2. If you used one of the Lectora provided Flash animations and need to make changes, click on the Flash Parameters icon.

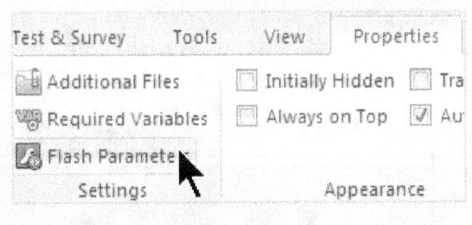

This opens a window where you can set the parameters.

3. As with other windows like this, you can delete rows by clicking on the ⊖.

4. You may want to change other settings using the Additional Files or Required Variables properties if your custom Flash animation requires it.

YouTube

You can easily insert links to YouTube videos with this tool. Just click and enter your URL.

Buttons

Buttons are a little easier to create now. You click one place on the Insert ribbon and create the desired button.

Text Buttons

The Text Button Wizard is easier to use and it allows you to justify the button text left, right, or center.

If you want to change the text in a button, you do it on the Properties ribbon. If needed, you can click the resize icon to have the button automatically fit the text you have in the button.

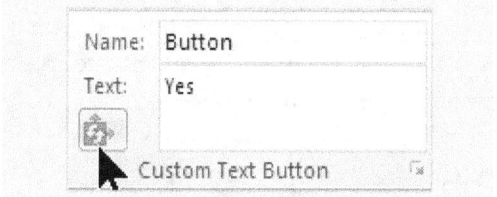

One thing that has changed about text buttons is that if you change the text in one button, other copies of the button will *not* change. Lectora automatically creates a new instance of the button and renames it.

> **Lectora 11 Tip 6:** To create a new button with the same look and feel as an existing one, just copy an existing button and paste it where you want the new button. Then change the text.

Okay, that is the good news. Now, what do you do if you want to change all instances of a text button? Say you had a button that said, "Check My Answer" that you had used many places in your course. Now your boss tells you to change it to "Check Answer." How do you change them all? Here are the steps.

Step	Example
1. In Lectora, copy the current button (Check My Answer) and paste on a new page say in a chapter used only for development.	Check My Answer

2.	Now change that button as needed and save your course.	Check Answer
3.	Now, in windows, open the images folder and sort by Date Modified (time) and look for the last button created. It usually is the name of the original button with 001 added on to it.	Your original button was most likely named change_my_answer.gif. Your copy will be change_my_answer001.gif.
4.	Make a copy of that button *in Windows*.	Copy of change_my_answer001.gif
5.	Then find the original button that you want to change and make sure you have its name. Delete it.	Delete change_my_answer.gif.
6.	Then rename the copy you just made of the changed button to the original one.	Rename Copy of change_my_answer001.gif to change_my_answer.gif.

Transparent Buttons

Transparent buttons now appear a partially transparent blue gray in Edit mode so you can position and size them. When your course is running, they are transparent.

Table of Contents

Now you can control what is shown in the Table of Contents by checking the boxes next to the Chapters, Sections, and Pages on the Properties ribbon. This is much easier than going to each page and checking it on the page properties.

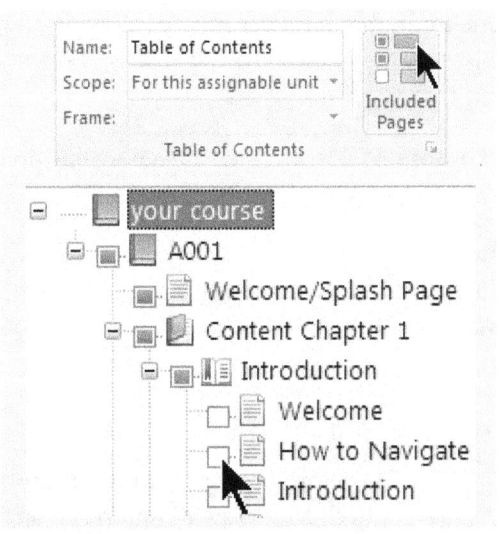

Menus

The Menu wizard now has a Preview pane which shows you what your formatting will look like without having to apply the properties changes.

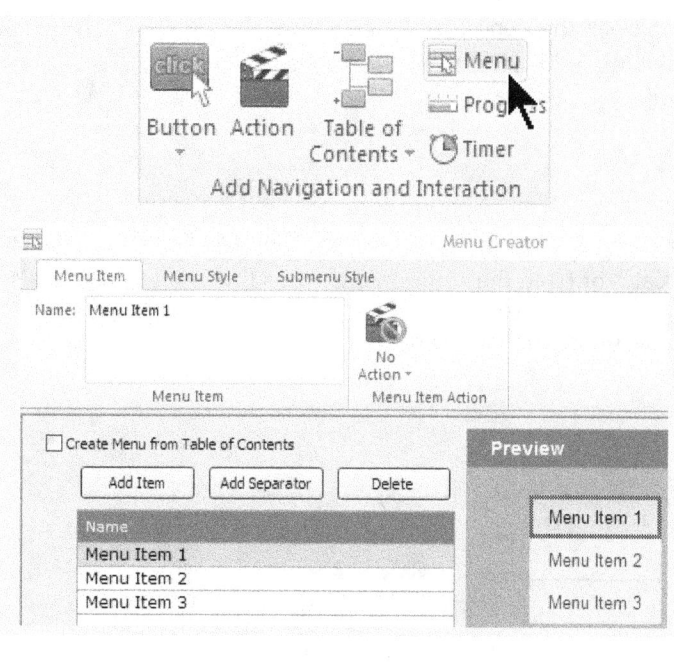

You can easily create a simple menu for course navigation by checking the Create Menu from Table of Contents. Then click the boxes next to any Chapter or Section you do *not* want to appear in your menu.

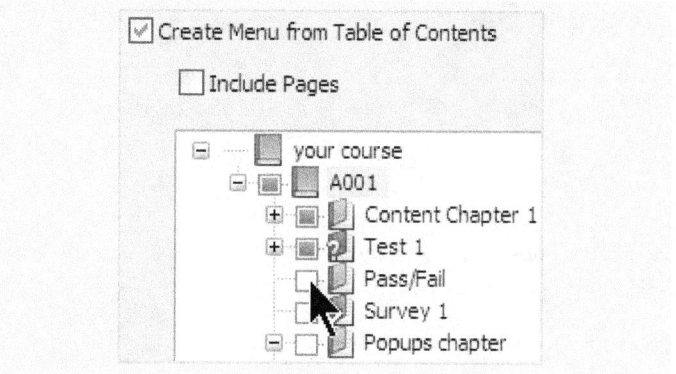

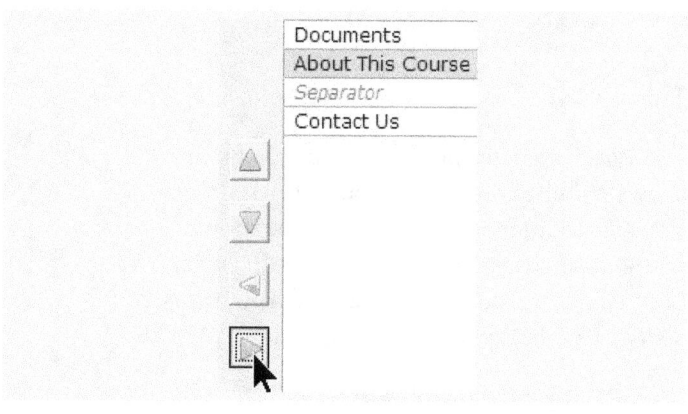

You move items around using the green arrows.

After you have created a menu, you can open the Menu Creator again by clicking on its icon on the Properties ribbon for the Menu.

You can change many options for the Menu Style and Submenu Style from either inside the Menu Creator or from the additional ribbons that appear when a Menu object is selected.

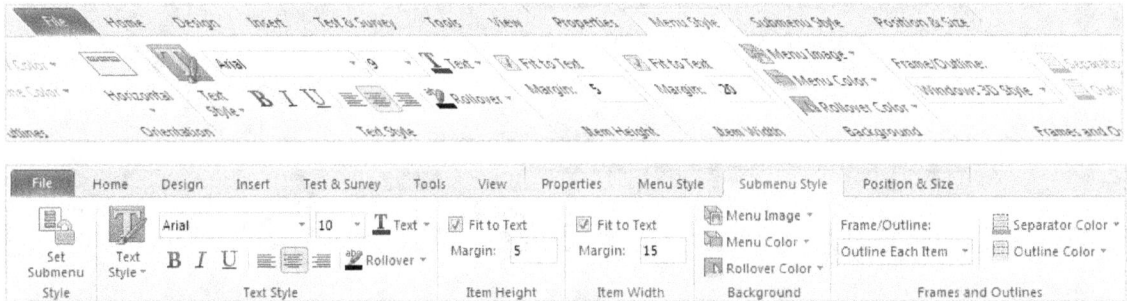

Progress Bar

For a Progress Bar,

you can now specify the desired Border Weight and Border color on the Properties ribbon.

Timer

The Timer is a new object. It is a text box that shows either a count up or count down timer. You set the interval and what is to be shown on the properties ribbon. It comes with an On Done Playing action that you can set. You can also add other On Done Playing actions.

Web Window

Not exactly sure what you use these for but you can have a window into the web.

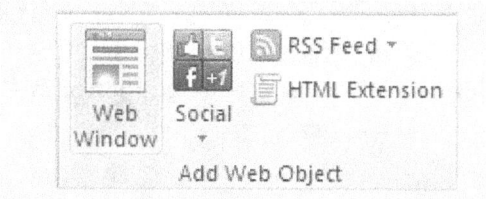

Social Media

If you have a community of practice, you might want to consider using one or more of these social media tools or the RSS Feed tool.

HTML Extension

The placeholder for and HTML object is now less confusing.

You edit the contents by clicking on the Edit icon on the Properties ribbon. You have a nice big window to edit your text in now.

And, on the Properties ribbon, you can now specify variables that are to be made available with the HTML.

QR Code

Finally, if your training involves QR codes, there is a way to easily access them. See the User Guide PDF for a complete description of this new addition.

Lectora Library

Your objects are now readily available by clicking My Library and then opening the Library Objects folder.

Insert a Library Object

Click on the My Library tab on the right side of the layout pane. It will open and you can just double click on the Library Object you want and it will be inserted.

Position & Size Ribbon

The Position & Size ribbon contains all the properties that used to be on Position and Size tab of the old Properties window.

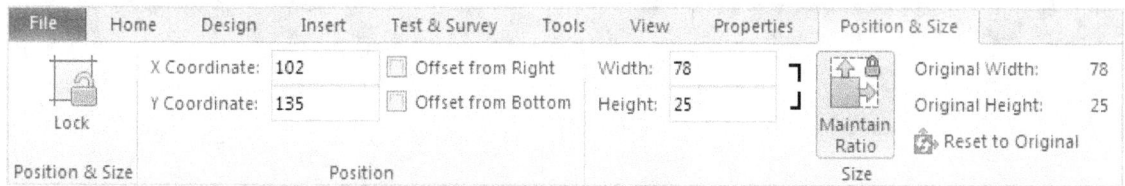

Properties

The properties ribbon contains whatever was on the General tab of the old Properties window.

Now you can change properties of multiple objects at one time.

> **Lectora 11 Tip 7:** One of the nice new things with Lectora 11 is that you can select multiple objects and change the *common properties* of all of them at the same time.
> – For text objects you can change all the font characteristics at one time.
> – For several Lectora shapes, you can change the color, border, etc. at one time.
> – For a mixed set of shapes, you can only change the properties that they have in common.

Test & Survey Ribbon

The Test & Survey ribbon lets you add tests, surveys, questions, and forms into your course. You can also add these from the Quick Insert group on the Home ribbon. Most things are the same with different icons with the exception of the questions where there have been many improvements.

If you don't see your question listed, then it had little change.

Choice Properties Common to Most Questions

Most questions have the following things in common in the Choices area.

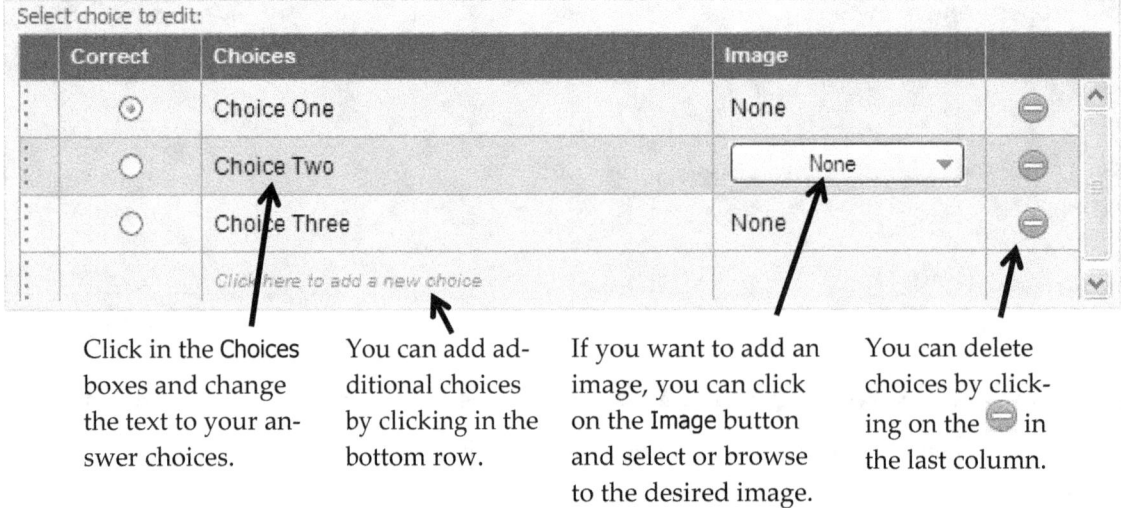

Click in the **Choices** boxes and change the text to your answer choices.

You can add additional choices by clicking in the bottom row.

If you want to add an image, you can click on the **Image** button and select or browse to the desired image.

You can delete choices by clicking on the ⊖ in the last column.

Drag and Drop Questions

Drag and Drop questions have been greatly improved.

- As with the matching question, you can now give text names to the answers that will appear in the answers shown on the **Results** pages in a test.
- Each **Drag** item may now have one *or more correct drop zones*. This allows you to have multiple items dropped in any order into any number of correct locations.
- Drop zones are independent of the drag items. You can make them any size you want and position them precisely by clicking on the ▢ icon on the right (not shown).

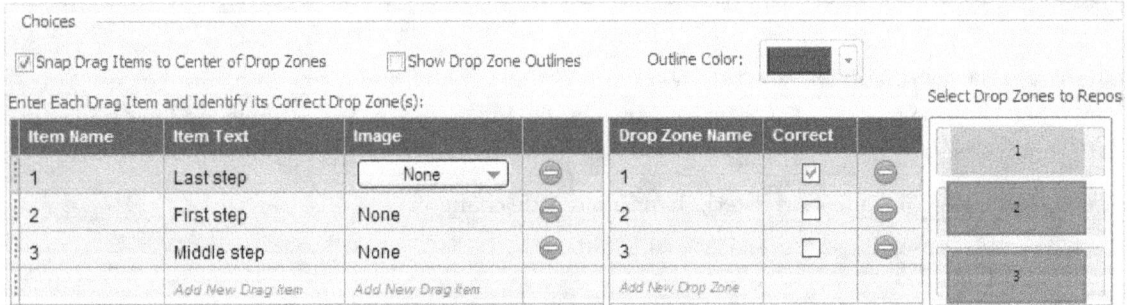

Lectora 11 Tip 8: This is now a very useful question for teaching concepts – what are and what are not examples of a given concept. For example, you could have two bowls for drop zones and several different fruits and vegetables. The learner would drag the fruits to one bowl and the vegetables to the other.

Lectora 11 Tip 9: Another great aspect of the changes is the ability to name the drag items and drop zones instead of relying on numbers. Now, you can give feedback much more easily. For example, if you name the drag items (apple, carrot) and name the drop zones (fruit, vege) in the question creator, then you can have actions to display feedback like "An apple is a fruit, not a vegetable" with a meaningful condition like "Question_0005 Contains apple-fruit" instead of an obscure condition like "Question_0005 Contains 1-2".

Hot Spot Questions

The big improvement in the hot spot question from previous versions of Lectora is that now, instead of just radio buttons, you can have rectangular transparent areas like transparent buttons.

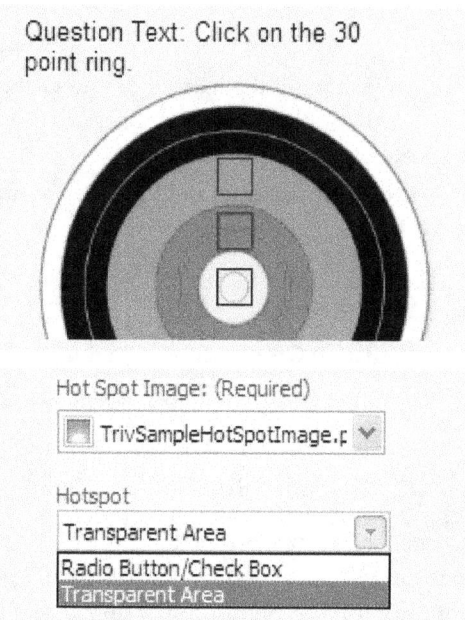

In the question properties you specify the image that will have the hot spots and the kind of hot spots you want.

You can make the hot spots any size you want and position them precisely by clicking on the icon on the right in the Choices area.

Lectora 11 Tip 10: Use this new capability to have students click on a map to identify locations or a process to identify key steps.

Fill in the Blank Questions

Fill in the Blank questions have been greatly improved.

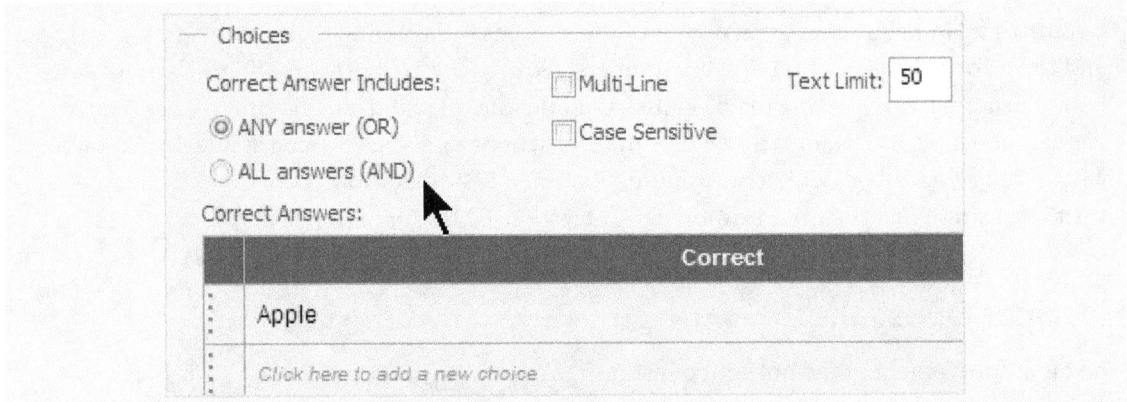

a. If you want the learner to enter one of the correct choices *exactly* including extra spaces and punctuation select ANY answer. If you simply want all the choices to be present in the answer regardless of punctuation or surrounding letters, select All answers. For example, if the correct answer is aaa then ANY requires aaa and only aaa to be correct while ALL considers bAaac to be correct.
b. If you want the learner to be able to press the enter key and enter multiple lines, check the Multi-Line box.
c. Turn on Case Sensitive if that matters.
d. Set the Text Limit to as near as you can to the entry length.

Matching Questions

Matching questions now offer more capabilities than previous versions in Lectora. You specify not only the text and optional image that is to appear in the matching pairs, but you can now specify

- the names that will appear in the answer variable and
- the color and width of the lines.

The Names default to 1, 2, 3, ... but you can change them to anything you want.

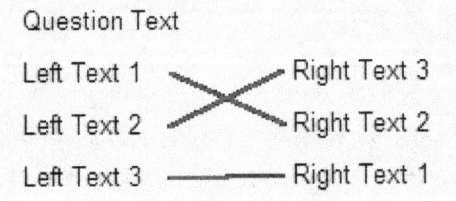

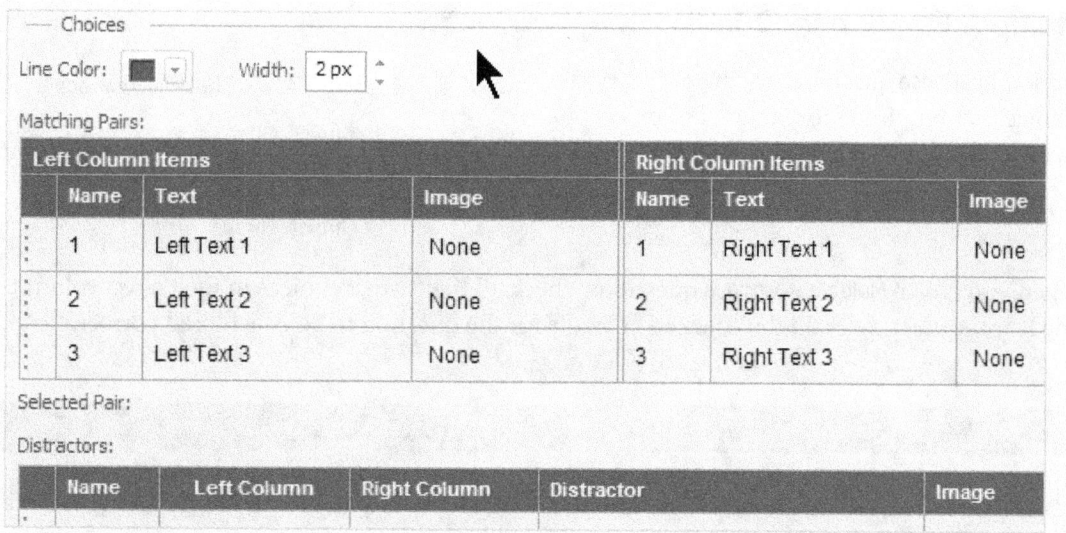

Multiple Choice Questions

The way you set this question up has changed dramatically for the better.

In the Choices area:

a. If you want the answer choices reordered each time the learner visits the page, check the Randomize choices box.

b. Indicate the correct answer by clicking the appropriate radio button in the Correct column.

c. If you want the answer choices listed in a dropdown list instead of all being shown at once on the page, check the Show choices as droplist box.

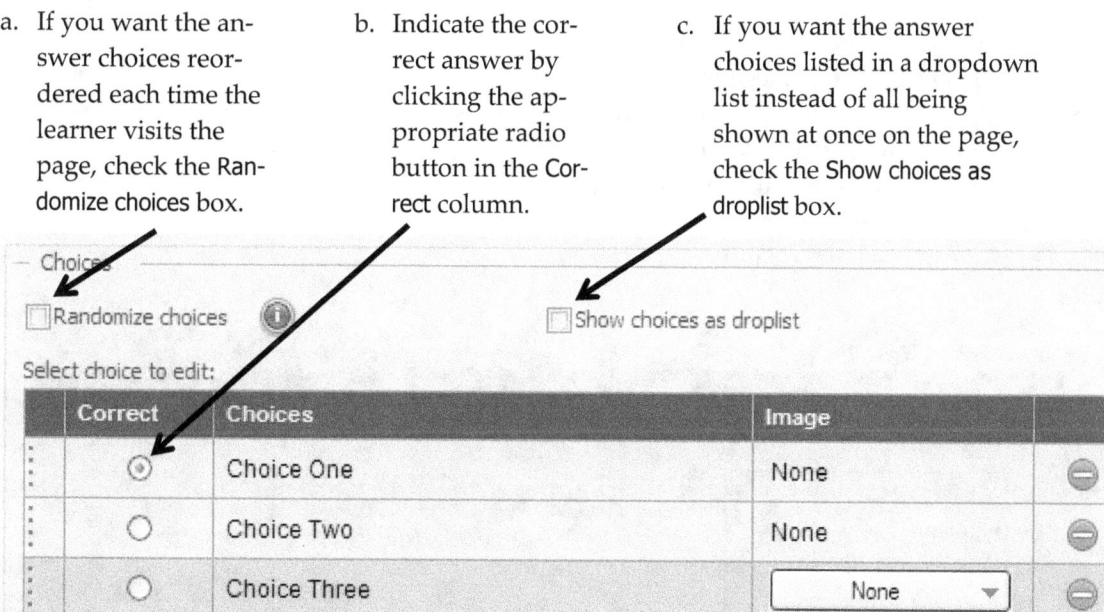

Lectora 11 Tip 11: You can now randomize the sequence in which the choices appear whenever this Randomize choices checkbox appears. This is another way to reduce cheating.

Multiple Response Questions

Multiple Response questions are the old Multiple Choice that required more than one correct answer. This is a much better name.

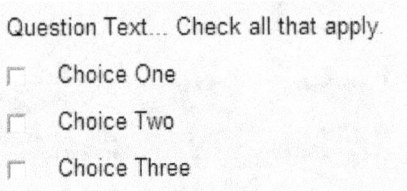

When you create Multiple Response questions, check all the correct choices in the Correct column. The learner must check *all* the checked answers for the question to be considered correct.

Number Entry Questions

Number Entry questions are new and are a special form of the Fill in the Blank question. They are good when you want to allow the entry of numeric answers that must fall within certain criteria. You specify the rules the number must satisfy to be considered correct. You can require that the answer satisfy any one of the rules or all of the rules.

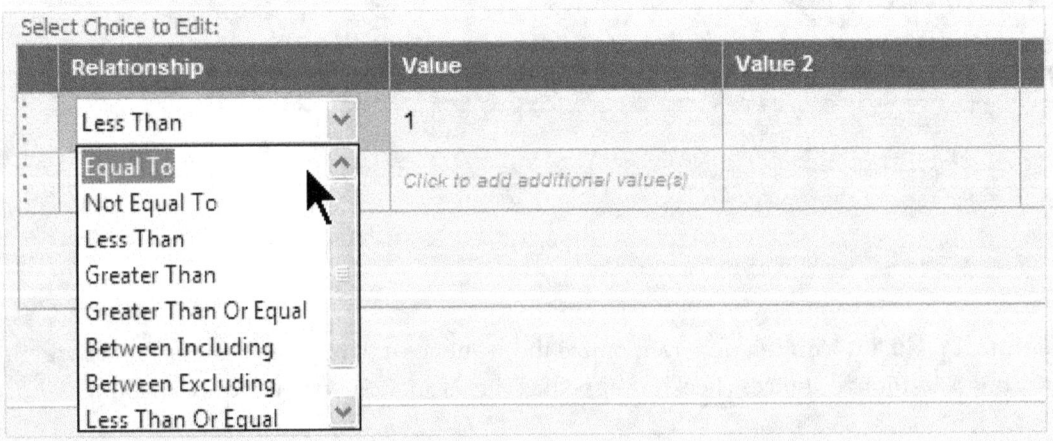

Rank/Sequence Questions

Rank/Sequence questions used to be just Survey questions but now you can use them in exercises and tests. The question gives learners a list of choices and has them indicate the proper order depending on the option you select.

- If you go with the default and leave the Show Choices In Droplist option unchecked, learners indicate the correct order by selecting the sequence number from dropdown list as shown here.

- If you check the Show Choices In Droplist, then the actual choices show up in the dropdown lists.

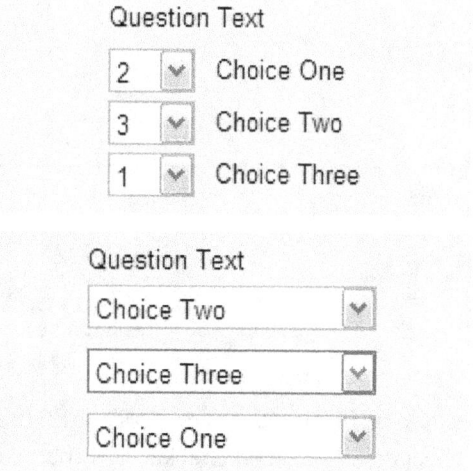

Lectora 11 Tip 12: Your question is much more memorable if you use the second option. The correct answer shows the objects in the proper sequence which imprints more effectively on the brain. The default option is not very memorable as well as being more prone to mistakes.

Question Feedback

To provide feedback, begin by clicking on the Feedback tab in the Question Creator and check Enable Feedback. If you have already closed the Question Creator you can open it easily by clicking on Edit Feedback on the Question Properties ribbon.

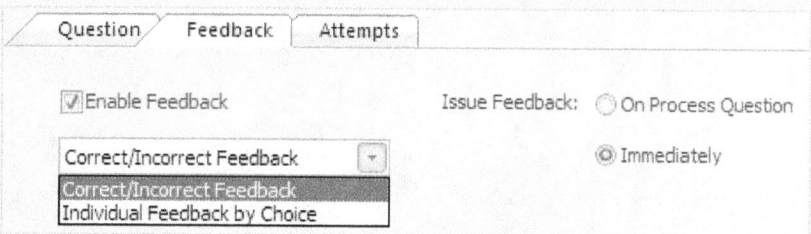

Once you have enabled feedback, the lower part of the Feedback page changes to allow you to create the kind of feedback you want. You click on one of the rows and it changes color to indicate that it is selected. Below these rows is an area where you can specify one action that will provide feedback. Normally this is Display Message.

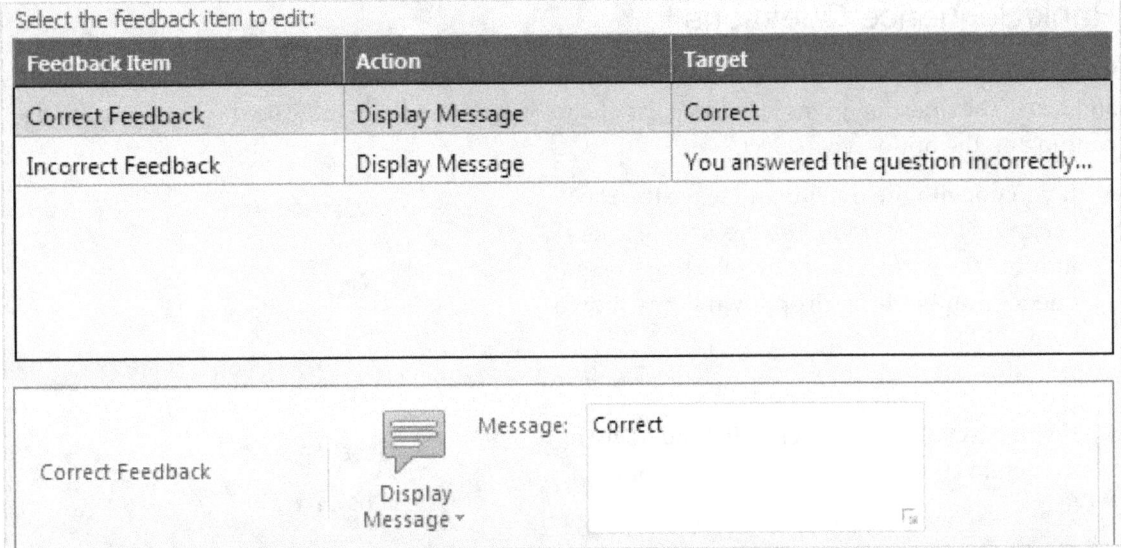

Lectora 11 Tip 13: As of April, 2013, the text in the Display Message action in a question is *not* checked by the spell checker. For that reason alone it is better to use hidden text blocks for correct and incorrect feedback *on the page* that are shown as needed.

Restricting the Number of Attempts

A brand new feature is now available to restrict the number of attempts.

On the Question Properties ribbon, you can easily see if feedback in enabled and how many attempts are allowed.

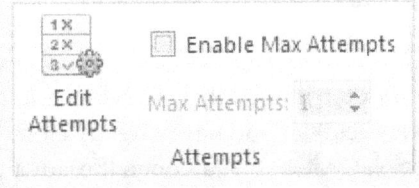

If you click the Edit Attempts icon, it opens the Attempts tab of the Question Creator.

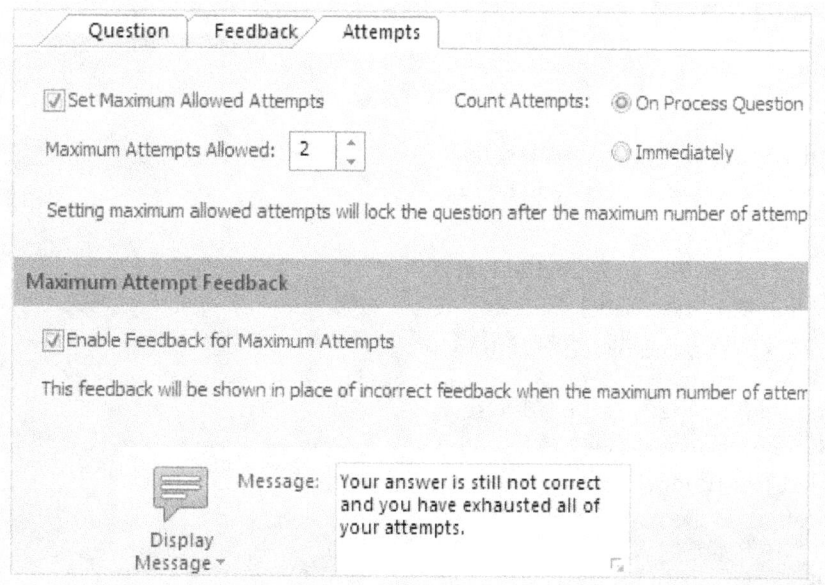

You can simply lock the question after the maximum attempts or you can lock it *and* give some feedback too.

Test Properties Ribbon

Tests really have *three* Properties ribbons, one for the usual Properties, one for how the Test behaves, and one for what and how results are shown.

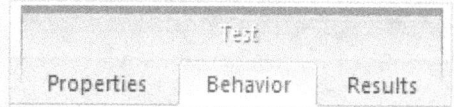

The Properties ribbon contains the same general properties as you would have for any other chapter.

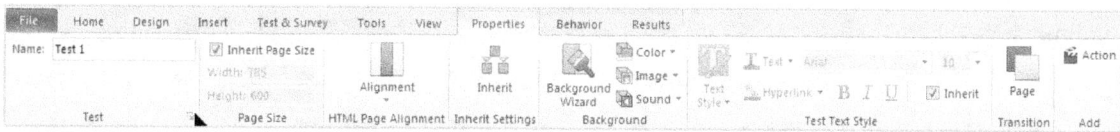

Test Behavior Ribbon

The Behavior ribbon controls how the test behaves during a test. It contains several of the tabs from the old Test properties window but nothing new.

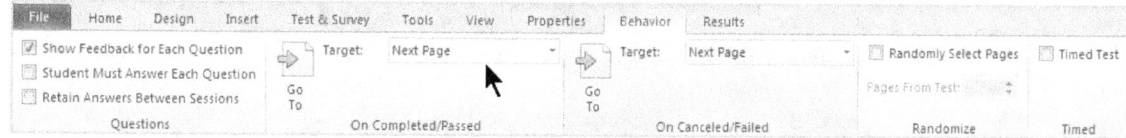

Timed Tests

1. If you want a timed test, check the last box. When the timer expires, the test will be processed which includes:
   - displaying the results you specified on the **Test Results** ribbon and
   - performing the passed or failed actions.

2. If you elected a timed test, you need to set how much time students have. Click on the newly added Test timer and drag it to the desired location on the page.

3. Then on its **Properties** ribbon, you can specify the amount of time in hours, minutes, and seconds as well as what will be shown in the timer.

4. In the **Style** group, you can specify the text properties of the timer.

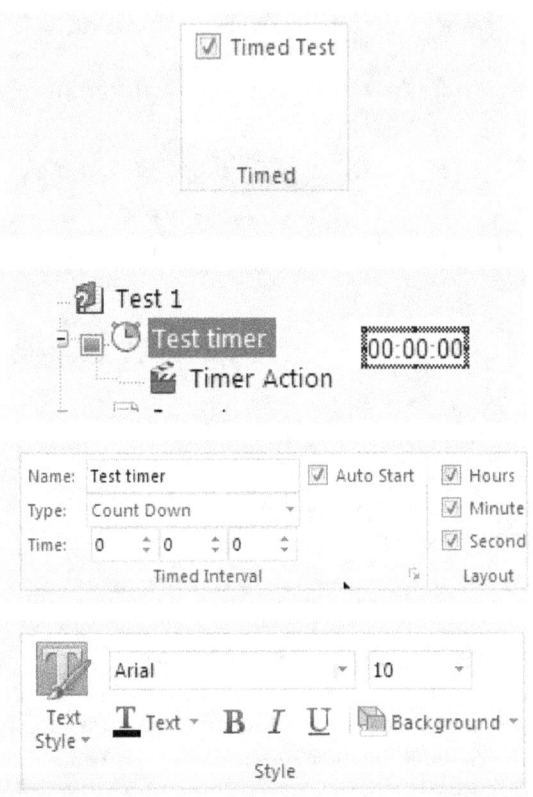

Test Results Ribbon

Not much new here.

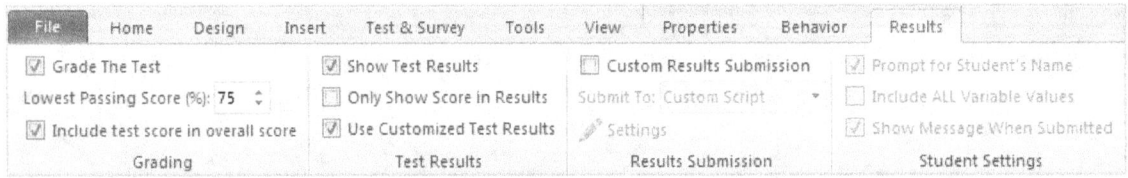

If you select **Use Customized Test Results**, then when you click on the **Test Results** page, you have an additional ribbon to specify what you want shown.

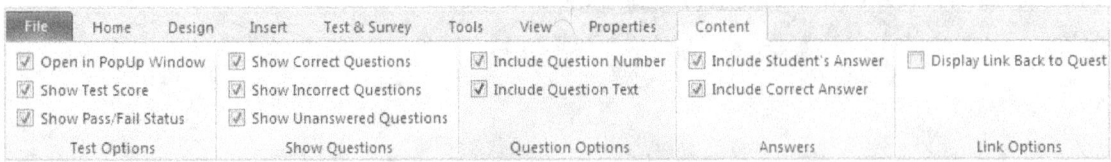

Tools Ribbon

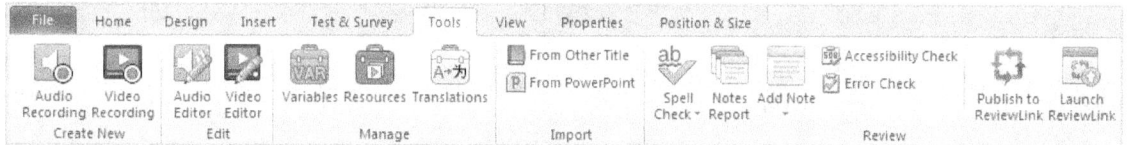

The Tools ribbon gives you tools to create and edit audio and video. You can find where specific variables and images are used in your course. This ribbon gives you access to Spell Check and Notes to document your course along with some tools to help when it comes time to have your course reviewed by others.

There is not much new here other than that you can record audio and video.

Recording Audio

Lectora provides a couple of ways you can record audio as long as you have a microphone on your computer.

- From the Tools ribbon, you can click on Audio Recording.

- You can open the Audio Editor by right clicking on any existing audio file and selecting Edit. There you can click on the record button next to the controller. It will open a dialog window where you can record your audio. You must have a microphone on your computer for this to work.

Recording Video

You can record your own video using Lectora but I don't recommend it. The qualities of most computer cameras (webcams) as well as the *recording environment* are *not* conducive to producing high quality video recordings.

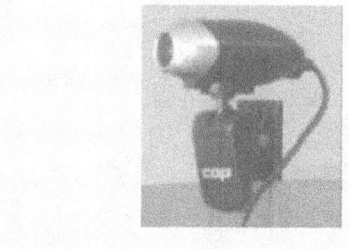

Lectora provides a couple of ways you can record audio as long as you have a microphone and a webcam on your computer.

View Ribbon

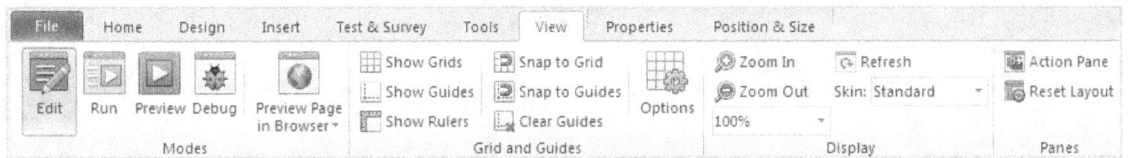

The View ribbon lets you see how your course will look and behave from the learner's perspective. It also gives you access to tools that help with layout like the Grid, Guides, and Zoom.

As you can see, the preferences relating to grids and guides are now on this ribbon.

Modes

This is the only place where you can run Debug mode in Lectora.

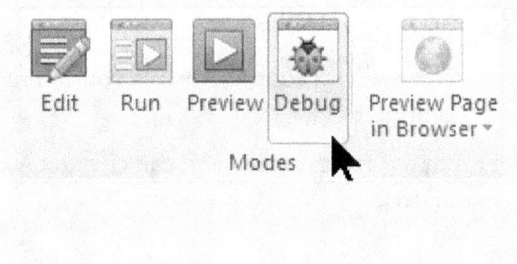

Grids and Guides

Now you easily clear all the guides by clicking on the Clear Guides icon. Be sure you want to do this because it cannot be undone.

To change the guide color, click on the Options icon and change it to a gray.

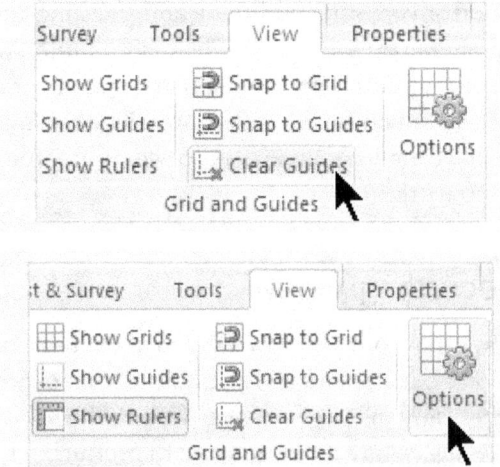

Refresh the Page

After moving things around and working extensively with a page, you may find that the layout is not what you expected. Before you panic, press F5 or click the Refresh icon in the Display group on the View ribbon. This will repaint the layout area as the learner will see it except for objects you have cleared the Visibility checkbox.

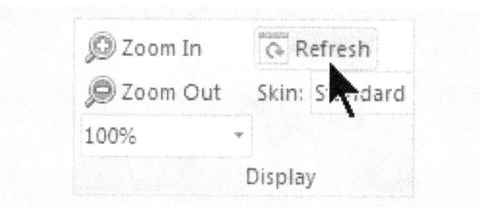

Moveable and Dockable Panes

The Action Pane and both views of the Title Explorer (Thumbnail View and Detail View) can be moved and docked in multiple places, including dragged onto a second monitor. If you want them back in their default locations, just click Reset Layout.

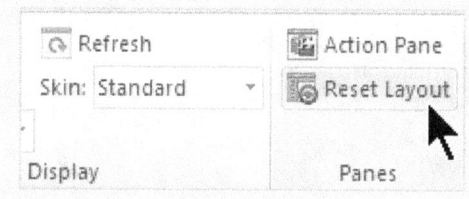

4. What Is the Downside?

What Did They Take Away?

- Actions inside buttons as one of the properties is gone. Now all actions are attached to the button. Good choice.

- Color code at cursor in status bar is gone. Not sure why they did this. Now, if you want to know the RGB color code for something, you have to do something like create a text box or shape and color it using the eyedropper. Then you can reopen the colors and go to Custom and you will see the codes there.

- You cannot put raw graphics in the library. You used to be able to put JPGs, PNGs, and GIFs in the Library by simply dragging them into the Library folder. You can still do that but when you click My Library, they are not visible.

- You cannot put a shortcut in the Library for the same reason. I used to have several different Libraries for different projects with shortcuts to the folders which were embedded in the project folders. Now I can create subfolders but they are not backed up nor are they part of the project folder like they used to be.

- There is no easy way to back up the Library now that shortcuts are gone. You used to be able to put objects in a subfolder of another folder that was already backed up. Then you had no worries. Now you have to make a special effort to backup Library objects.

- To create a new text button with similar properties to an existing one, you used to be able to just open an old button with the button wizard and go through it. Now, you copy an existing button and change the text. Just a different way to do the same thing.

What Doesn't Work As Expected or Needed

- With the introduction of the Breadcrumbs object, you would think there would be an option to check the page names. Nope. So, if you misspell a page name, it will not get caught.
- Spellcheck does not appear to be checking the answer choices if you select a Dropdown list. They are working on this one.
- Spellcheck does not appear to be checking the question feedback text. They are working on this one.
- Even though you have a nice option to create a menu from a TOC, you cannot create one for a chapter that just shows the sections at the top level. I put all my content in one chapter for page numbering purposes and then subdivide it into sections. Bummer.
- While you can string variables and text together in a single value field of an action, you cannot do math expressions this same way.
- You cannot change the standard color scheme like you can in PowerPoint.
- Once you have clicked OK in the question wizard and closed the window, you can still edit the question but you cannot change the question type other than switching between Multiple Choice and Multiple Response.

- Remember, if your Lectora window is not wide enough, many of the ribbons will not look like what you see in this book. You should expand the window as wide as it will go and then close it back up until just before groups start compressing.
- Remember getting this message when you published?

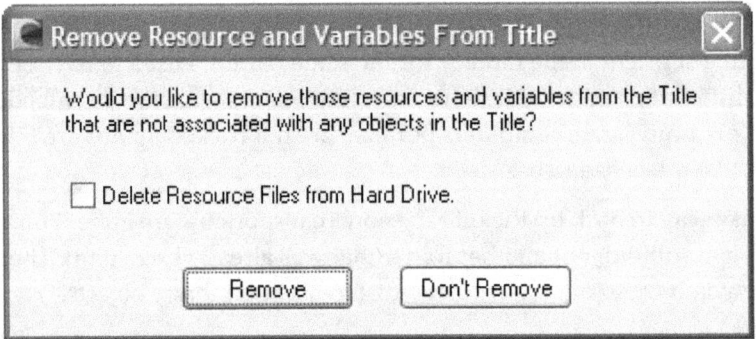

It was nice in that it if you checked the Delete box, it got rid of resources (graphics, SWFs, audios, videos, and attachments) that you no longer used. Well, it is gone. Now the old graphics stay around until you manually go to Windows and delete them. Reports are that they are working on this one too.

Lectora 11 Tip 14: One workaround for this is to first open the Resource Manager and remove the unused resources. Then go to the File tab and Export to a ZIP file. Then, after backing up the folder, delete the subfolders like extern, images, files, etc. Then replace them with the ones in the zip file.

Index

A
actions—13, 14, 15, 25, 44
animation—20
audio—21, 42
author control—16

B
bread crumbs—18
buttons—26

C
characters—20
color
   eyedropper—17
customize—11

D
Debug mode—43
description field—13
drag and drop question—33

E
edit—11

F
feedback - question—38
fill in the blank question—35
flash—25

G
graphics
   Lectora shapes—21

H
help—9
hot spot—34
hot spot question—34
HTML object—31

L
library—31

M
matching question—35
math—46
menus—28
modes—43
multiple choice question—36
multiple response questions—37

N
number entry question—37
number of attempts—39

P
page layout
   grids—43
   guides—43
pose-able characters—20
preferences—16
progress bar—30
properties—8, 32
properties - title—16

Q
QR Code—31
question feedback—38

questions—33
   feedback—39
Quick Access Toolbar—12

R
randomize—36
rank/sequence question—38
refresh—44
reset—44

S
save options—13, 16
shortcut keys—12
smart text—17
social media—30
spellcheck—46

T
table of contents—28

Table of Contents—28, 29
tables—18
test & survey—33
test behavior—40
test results—41
timer—30
toolbars to ribbons—8
tools—42

V
video—21, 42

W
web window—30

Y
YouTube—26

www.ingramcontent.com/pod-product-compliance
Lightning Source LLC
Chambersburg PA
CBHW081613170526
45166CB00009B/2950